# COCONUT

## more than 60 recipes

pil

Publications International, Ltd.

**Pictured on the front cover:** Coconut Cake *(page 100)*.

**Pictured on the back cover** *(left to right, top to bottom):* Piña Colada Milk Shake *(page 24)*, Amaretto Coconut Cream Pie *(page 110)*, Coconut Curry Chicken Soup *(page 52)*, Toasted Coconut Doughnuts *(page 12)*, Chocolate Macaroon Bars *(page 74)* and Tofu, Vegetable and Curry Stir-Fry *(page 44)*.

ISBN: 978-1-68022-791-8

Library of Congress Control Number: 2016960243

Manufactured in China.

8 7 6 5 4 3 2 1

**Microwave Cooking:** Microwave ovens vary in wattage. Use the cooking times as guidelines and check for doneness before adding more time.

# TABLE OF CONTENTS

# BREAKFAST & BREADS

## MAPLE PECAN GRANOLA

Makes about 13 cups

◇◇◇◇◇◇◇◇◇◇◇◇◇◇◇◇◇◇◇◇◇◇◇◇◇◇◇◇◇◇◇◇◇◇◇◇◇◇◇◇◇◇

½ cup maple syrup

½ cup packed dark brown sugar

1 tablespoon vanilla extract

1 teaspoon ground cinnamon

1 teaspoon kosher salt

¾ cup vegetable oil

6 cups old-fashioned rolled oats

½ cup ground flax seeds

1½ cups flaked coconut

3 cups pecans, coarsely chopped

**1.** Preheat oven to 350°F. Line two baking sheets with parchment paper. Set oven racks to upper third and lower third positions.

**2.** Whisk maple syrup, brown sugar, vanilla, cinnamon, salt and oil in large bowl. Stir in oats, flax seeds, coconut and pecans until evenly coated.

**3.** Divide mixture between prepared baking sheets, pressing granola into even layer. Bake 30 minutes or until mixture is golden brown and fragrant, stirring and rotating baking sheets from top to bottom. Let granola cool completely on baking sheets. Spoon evenly into jars, reserving extra for another use.

# BLUEBERRY COCONUT FLOUR MUFFINS

Makes 12 muffins

◇◇◇◇◇◇◇◇◇◇◇◇◇◇◇◇◇◇◇◇◇◇◇◇◇◇◇◇◇◇◇◇◇

| | |
|---|---|
| 6 | eggs |
| ½ | cup sugar |
| ¼ | cup (½ stick) butter, melted |
| ¼ | cup whole milk |
| ½ | cup plus 2 teaspoons coconut flour,* divided |
| 2 | teaspoons grated lemon peel |
| ½ | teaspoon salt |
| ½ | teaspoon baking powder |
| ½ | teaspoon xanthan gum |
| 1 | cup fresh blueberries |

*Coconut flour is a gluten-free, high fiber flour available in the specialty flour section of many supermarkets. It can also be ordered online.

1. Preheat oven to 375°F. Line 12 standard (2½-inch) muffin cups with paper baking cups.

2. Whisk eggs, sugar, butter and milk in medium bowl until well combined.

3. Mix ½ cup coconut flour, lemon peel, salt, baking powder and xanthan gum in medium bowl. Sift flour mixture into egg mixture. Whisk until batter is smooth.

4. Combine blueberries with remaining 2 teaspoons coconut flour in small bowl. Stir gently into batter. Pour evenly into prepared muffin cups.

5. Bake 12 to 15 minutes or until toothpick inserted into centers comes out clean. Cool in pan on wire rack 5 minutes. Remove from pan; serve warm.

# PUMPKIN GRANOLA

Makes about 5½ cups

3 cups old-fashioned oats

¾ cup coarsely chopped almonds

¾ cup raw pumpkin seeds (pepitas)

½ cup canned pumpkin

½ cup maple syrup

⅓ cup coconut oil, melted

1 teaspoon vanilla

1 teaspoon ground cinnamon

½ teaspoon salt

¼ teaspoon ground ginger

¼ teaspoon ground nutmeg

Pinch ground cloves

¾ cup dried cranberries

1. Preheat oven to 325°F. Line large rimmed baking sheet with parchment paper.

2. Combine oats, almonds and pumpkin seeds in large bowl. Combine pumpkin, maple syrup, oil, vanilla, cinnamon, salt, ginger, nutmeg and cloves in medium bowl; stir until well blended. Pour over oat mixture; stir until well blended and all ingredients are completely coated. Spread mixture evenly on prepared baking sheet.

3. Bake 50 to 60 minutes or until granola is golden brown and no longer moist, stirring every 20 minutes. (Granola will become more crisp as it cools.) Stir in cranberries; cool completely.

Variations: For Pumpkin Chocolate Granola, follow recipe above but reduce amount of maple syrup to ⅓ cup. Stir in ¾ cup semisweet chocolate chips after baking. You can substitute pecans or walnuts for the almonds, and/or add ¾ cup flaked coconut to the mixture before baking.

# LOADED BANANA BREAD

### Makes 1 loaf (about 12 servings)

◇◇◇◇◇◇◇◇◇◇◇◇◇◇◇◇◇◇◇◇◇◇◇◇◇◇◇◇◇◇◇◇◇◇◇◇

½  **cup (1 stick) butter, softened**

½  **cup granulated sugar**

½  **cup packed brown sugar**

2  **eggs**

1½  **cups mashed bananas (about 3 ripe bananas)**

¼  **cup sour cream**

½  **teaspoon vanilla**

1½  **cups all-purpose flour**

2½  **teaspoons baking powder**

¼  **teaspoon salt**

1  **can (8 ounces) crushed pineapple, drained**

⅓  **cup flaked coconut**

¼  **cup mini semisweet chocolate chips**

1. Preheat oven to 350°F. Spray 9×5-inch loaf pan with nonstick cooking spray.

2. Beat butter, granulated sugar and brown sugar in large bowl with electric mixer at medium speed until light and fluffy. Beat in eggs, one at a time, scraping down bowl after each addition. Add bananas, sour cream and vanilla. Beat just until combined.

3. Sift flour, baking powder and salt in small bowl. Gradually beat flour mixture into banana mixture just until combined. Fold in pineapple, coconut and chocolate chips. Spoon batter into prepared pan.

4. Bake 50 minutes or until toothpick inserted into center comes out almost clean. Cool in pan 1 hour; remove from pan.

# TOASTED COCONUT DOUGHNUTS

Makes 14 to 16 doughnuts

〈〉〈〉〈〉〈〉〈〉〈〉〈〉〈〉〈〉〈〉〈〉〈〉〈〉〈〉〈〉〈〉〈〉〈〉〈〉〈〉〈〉〈〉〈〉〈〉

2¾ cups all-purpose flour

¼ cup cornstarch

1½ teaspoons baking powder

1 teaspoon salt

½ teaspoon ground cinnamon

½ teaspoon ground nutmeg

1 cup granulated sugar

2 eggs

¼ cup (½ stick) butter, melted

¼ cup applesauce

1 teaspoon vanilla

¾ cup unsweetened canned coconut milk, divided*

Vegetable oil for frying

1 teaspoon dark rum or vanilla

1½ cups sifted powdered sugar

1 cup flaked coconut, toasted**

*Shake the can vigorously to blend before opening the can, or pour contents of can into bowl and whisk to combine.

**Spread coconut in large skillet; cook over medium-low heat about 10 minutes or until mostly golden brown, stirring frequently.

1. Whisk flour, cornstarch, baking powder, salt, cinnamon and nutmeg in large bowl.

2. Beat 1 cup granulated sugar and eggs in large bowl with electric mixer on high speed 3 minutes or until pale and thick. Stir in butter, applesauce and vanilla. Add flour mixture alternately with ½ cup coconut milk, mixing on low speed after each addition. Press plastic wrap directly onto surface of dough; refrigerate at least 1 hour.

3. Pour about 2 inches of oil into Dutch oven or large heavy saucepan; clip deep-fry or candy thermometer to side of pot. Heat over medium-high heat to 360°F to 370°F.

4. Meanwhile, generously flour work surface. Turn out dough onto work surface and dust top with flour. Roll dough about ¼-inch thick; cut out donuts with floured donut cutter. Gather and reroll scraps. Line large wire rack with paper towels.

5. Working in batches, add donuts to hot oil. Cook 1 minute per side or until golden brown. Do not crowd the pan and adjust heat to maintain temperature during frying. Drain on prepared wire racks.

6. Whisk remaining ¼ cup coconut milk and rum in medium bowl. Whisk in powdered sugar to form smooth, thick glaze. Dip tops of donuts in glaze, letting excess drip back into bowl; immediately dip in coconut. Let stand until glaze is set.

# CHERRY-COCONUT-CHEESE COFFEECAKE

### Makes 10 servings

2½ cups all-purpose flour

¾ cup sugar

½ teaspoon baking powder

½ teaspoon baking soda

6 ounces cream cheese, softened, divided

¾ cup milk

2 tablespoons coconut or vegetable oil

2 eggs, divided

1 teaspoon vanilla

½ cup flaked coconut

¾ cup cherry preserves

2 tablespoons butter

**1.** Preheat oven to 350°F. Grease and flour 9-inch springform pan.

**2.** Combine flour and sugar in large bowl. Reserve ½ cup flour mixture; set aside. Stir baking powder and baking soda into remaining flour mixture. Cut in half of cream cheese with pastry blender or two knives until mixture resembles coarse crumbs; set aside.

**3.** Combine milk, oil and 1 egg in medium bowl. Add to cream cheese mixture; stir just until moistened. Spread batter on bottom and 1 inch up side of prepared pan. Combine remaining cream cheese, egg and vanilla in small bowl; whisk until smooth. Pour over batter, spreading to within 1 inch of edge. Sprinkle coconut over cream cheese mixture. Spoon preserves evenly over coconut.

**4.** Cut butter into reserved flour mixture with pastry blender or two knives until mixture resembles coarse crumbs. Sprinkle over preserves.

**5.** Bake 55 to 60 minutes or until golden brown and toothpick inserted into crust comes out clean. Cool in pan on wire rack 15 minutes. Remove side of pan; serve warm.

# MINI COCONUT ORANGE ROLLS

Makes 24 rolls

⋄⋄⋄⋄⋄⋄⋄⋄⋄⋄⋄⋄⋄⋄⋄⋄⋄⋄⋄⋄⋄⋄⋄⋄⋄⋄⋄⋄⋄⋄⋄⋄⋄⋄⋄⋄⋄⋄⋄⋄⋄⋄⋄

¾ **cup plus 2 tablespoons milk**

⅓ **cup plus 2 tablespoons butter, divided**

2⅔ **to 3 cups bread flour, divided**

½ **cup plus ⅓ cup sugar, divided**

1 **package (¼ ounce) rapid-rise active dry yeast**

1 **tablespoon grated orange peel, divided**

¾ **teaspoon salt**

½ **cup flaked coconut**

⅓ **cup orange juice**

2 **tablespoons corn syrup**

1. Combine milk and ⅓ cup butter in small saucepan; heat to 120°F. Whisk 1 cup flour, ¼ cup sugar, yeast, 1 teaspoon grated orange peel and salt in large bowl of electric stand mixer. Add milk mixture; beat at medium speed 2 minutes.

2. Attach dough hook to mixer; beat in enough remaining flour until firm dough forms. Knead at medium-low speed 5 minutes or until smooth and elastic. Place dough in greased bowl; turn to grease top. Cover and let rise in warm place about 30 minutes or until doubled.

3. Spray 24 mini (1¾-inch) muffin cups with nonstick cooking spray. Combine ¼ cup sugar and remaining 2 teaspoons grated orange peel in small bowl. Divide dough in half; roll out each half into 12×6-inch rectangle on lightly floured surface. Melt remaining 2 tablespoons butter; spread 1 tablespoon butter over each rectangle. Sprinkle evenly with sugar mixture and coconut. Starting with long side, roll up tightly jelly-roll style; pinch seams to seal. Cut crosswise into 1-inch slices; place slices, cut sides up, in prepared muffin cups. Cover and let rise in warm place about 20 minutes or until doubled. Preheat oven to 375°F.

4. Bake about 25 minutes or until golden brown. Remove to wire racks; cool 5 minutes. Combine orange juice and corn syrup in small saucepan. Bring to a boil. Reduce heat; simmer 3 minutes. Brush over warm rolls.

# PIÑA COLADA MUFFINS

## Makes 18 muffins

◇◇◇◇◇◇◇◇◇◇◇◇◇◇◇◇◇◇◇◇◇◇◇◇◇◇◇◇◇◇◇◇◇◇◇◇◇◇

2 cups all-purpose flour

¾ cup sugar

¾ cup flaked coconut, divided

2 teaspoons baking powder

½ teaspoon baking soda

½ teaspoon salt

2 eggs

1 cup sour cream

1 can (8 ounces) crushed pineapple in juice, undrained

¼ cup (½ stick) butter, melted

⅛ teaspoon coconut extract

1. Preheat oven to 400°F. Line 18 standard (2½-inch) muffin cups with paper baking cups or spray with nonstick cooking spray.

2. Combine flour, sugar, ½ cup coconut, baking powder, baking soda and salt in large bowl; mix well.

3. Beat eggs in medium bowl with electric mixer at medium speed 1 to 2 minutes or until frothy. Beat in sour cream, pineapple with juice, butter and coconut extract. Stir into flour mixture just until combined. Spoon batter into prepared muffin cups, filling three-fourths full.

4. Bake 15 to 20 minutes or until toothpick inserted into centers comes out clean, sprinkling with remaining ¼ cup coconut after 10 minutes. If desired, sprinkle tops of muffins with additional coconut after first 10 minutes. Cool in pans 2 minutes. Remove to wire racks; cool completely.

# COCONUT BUTTERSCOTCH DOUGHNUTS

Makes 12 doughnuts

◇◇◇◇◇◇◇◇◇◇◇◇◇◇◇◇◇◇◇◇◇◇◇◇◇◇◇◇◇◇◇◇◇◇◇

| | |
|---|---|
| 1 | cup all-purpose flour |
| ½ | cup sugar |
| 2 | tablespoons cornstarch |
| 1½ | teaspoons baking powder |
| ½ | teaspoon baking soda |
| ½ | teaspoon salt |
| ½ | cup buttermilk |
| ¼ | cup (½ stick) butter, melted |
| 1 | egg |
| ½ | teaspoon vanilla |
| ¼ | cup flaked coconut |
| ¼ | cup butterscotch chips |

◇◇◇◇◇◇◇◇◇◇◇◇◇◇◇◇◇◇◇◇◇

## Topping

| | |
|---|---|
| ¼ | cup whipping cream |
| ½ | cup butterscotch chips |
| ½ | cup flaked coconut, toasted* |
| ¼ | cup bittersweet chocolate chips, melted |

*To toast coconut, spread in single layer in heavy-bottomed skillet. Cook and stir over medium heat 2 to 3 minutes or until lightly browned. Remove from skillet; cool completely.

1. Preheat oven to 425°F. Spray 12 cavities of donut pan with nonstick cooking spray.

2. Combine flour, sugar, cornstarch, baking powder, baking soda and salt in medium bowl; mix well. Whisk buttermilk, butter, egg and vanilla in medium bowl until well blended. Stir into flour mixture just until blended. Fold in ¼ cup coconut and ¼ cup butterscotch chips.

3. Spoon batter into medium resealable food storage bag. Cut ½-inch corner from bag. Pipe mixture evenly into prepared cups, filling half full.

4. Bake about 7 minutes or until donuts are puffed and golden. Cool in pan on wire rack 3 to 5 minutes. Remove to wire rack; cool completely.

5. For glaze, heat cream in small saucepan over medium-low heat until bubbles form around edge of pan. Add ½ cup butterscotch chips; whisk until melted and smooth. Let cool slightly. Dip tops of donuts in glaze; place on wire rack. Dip tops again; immediately sprinkle with toasted coconut. Drizzle with melted chocolate.

# DRINKS

## COCONUT MILKSHAKE
Makes 1 serving

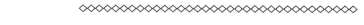

1  **tablespoon honey, divided**

3  **tablespoons flaked coconut, divided**

1  **cup coconut sorbet**

½  **cup unsweetened canned coconut milk**

¼  **cup crushed ice**

1. Dip rim of glass into ½ tablespoon honey; dip into 1 tablespoon flaked coconut.

2. Combine sorbet, coconut milk, ice, remaining 2 tablespoons flaked coconut and ½ tablespoon honey in blender; blend until smooth. Pour into prepared glass; serve immediately.

# PIÑA COLADA MILKSHAKE

◇◇◇◇◇◇◇◇◇◇◇◇◇◇◇◇◇◇◇◇◇◇◇◇◇◇◇◇◇◇◇◇◇◇◇◇

2 cups (1 pint) coconut
   sorbet

2 cups (1 pint) vanilla
   frozen yogurt or ice
   cream

¾ cup pineapple juice

¼ cup dark rum or
   ½ teaspoon rum
   extract

1. Combine sorbet, frozen yogurt, pineapple juice and rum in blender. Process until smooth.

2. Pour into four glasses. Serve immediately.

# BANANA-COCONUT "CREAM PIE" SMOOTHIE

### Makes 4 servings

3 bananas, sliced

1½ cups unsweetened canned coconut milk, chilled

1½ cups pineapple juice, chilled

2 tablespoons sugar

½ teaspoon vanilla

⅛ teaspoon ground nutmeg

3 ice cubes

Shredded coconut, toasted* (optional)

*To toast coconut, spread in single layer in heavy-bottomed skillet. Cook and stir over medium heat 2 to 3 minutes or until lightly browned. Remove from skillet; cool completely.*

**1.** Combine bananas, coconut milk, pineapple juice, sugar, vanilla, nutmeg and ice in blender; blend until smooth.

**2.** Pour into four glasses. Garnish with toasted coconut.

# MAIN DISHES

## THAI CURRIED VEGETABLES

Makes 4 to 6 servings

◇◇◇◇◇◇◇◇◇◇◇◇◇◇◇◇◇◇◇◇◇◇◇◇◇◇◇◇◇◇◇◇◇◇◇◇◇◇◇◇◇

1  can (about 13 ounces) unsweetened coconut milk

1  tablespoon Thai red curry paste

½  teaspoon salt

1  bag (16 ounces) frozen Asian vegetable mixture, such as broccoli, carrots and water chestnuts

4  to 6 cups hot cooked rice

Slivered fresh basil

**1.** Combine coconut milk, curry paste and salt in large saucepan. Cook and stir over medium-high heat 5 minutes.

**2.** Add vegetables and bring to a boil. Cover; reduce heat to medium and cook until vegetables are crisp-tender, stirring occasionally. Serve over rice topped with basil, if desire.

# BAKED FISH WITH THAI PESTO

Makes 4 to 6 servings

1 to 2 jalapeño peppers, seeded and coarsely chopped

1 lemon

4 green onions, thinly sliced

2 tablespoons chopped fresh ginger

3 cloves garlic, minced

1½ cups lightly packed fresh basil leaves

1 cup lightly packed fresh cilantro leaves

¼ cup lightly packed fresh mint leaves

¼ cup roasted peanuts

¼ cup flaked coconut

½ teaspoon sugar

½ cup peanut oil

2 pounds boneless fish fillets (such as salmon, halibut, cod or orange roughy)

Lemon and cucumber slices

1. Place jalapeño peppers in blender or food processor.

2. Grate peel of lemon. Juice lemon to measure 2 tablespoons. Add peel and juice to blender.

3. Add green onions, ginger, garlic, basil, cilantro, mint, peanuts, coconut and sugar to blender; blend until finely chopped. With motor running, slowly pour in oil; blend until mixed.

4. Preheat oven to 375°F. Rinse fish and pat dry with paper towels. Place fillets on lightly oiled baking sheet. Spread solid thin layer of pesto over each fillet.

5. Bake 10 minutes or until fish begins to flake when tested with fork and is just opaque in center. Transfer fish to serving platter with wide spatula. Garnish with lemon and cucumber slices.

# PUMPKIN CURRY

Makes 4 servings

1 tablespoon coconut oil

1 package (14 ounces) extra firm tofu, drained and cut into 1-inch cubes

¼ cup Thai red curry paste

2 cloves garlic, minced

1 can (15 ounces) pumpkin puree

1 can (about 13 ounces) unsweetened coconut milk

1 cup water

1½ teaspoons salt

1 teaspoon sriracha sauce

4 cups cut-up vegetables (broccoli, cauliflower, red bell pepper, sweet potato)

½ cup peas

2 cups hot cooked rice

¼ cup shredded fresh basil (optional)

1. Heat oil in wok or large skillet over high heat. Add tofu; stir-fry 2 to 3 minutes or until lightly browned. Add curry paste and garlic; cook and stir 1 minute or until tofu is coated. Add pumpkin, coconut milk, water, salt and sriracha; bring to a boil. Stir in vegetables.

2. Reduce heat to medium; cover and simmer 20 minutes or until vegetables are tender. Stir in peas; cook 1 minute or until heated through. Serve over rice; top with basil, if desired.

Note: Don't worry if the coconut milk looks separated. Just add it all to the wok and it will come together as it heats.

# THAI-STYLE CHICKEN THIGHS

Makes 6 servings

1 teaspoon ground ginger

½ teaspoon salt

¼ teaspoon ground red pepper

6 bone-in chicken thighs (about 2¼ pounds), skin removed

1 medium onion, chopped

3 cloves garlic, minced

⅓ cup unsweetened canned coconut milk

¼ cup peanut butter

2 tablespoons soy sauce

2 tablespoons water

1 tablespoon cornstarch

3 cups hot cooked couscous or yellow rice

¼ cup chopped fresh cilantro

Lime wedges (optional)

## Slow Cooker Directions

1. Combine ginger, salt and red pepper in small bowl; sprinkle over meaty sides of chicken. Place onion and garlic in slow cooker; top with chicken. Whisk together coconut milk, peanut butter and soy sauce; pour over chicken. Cover; cook on LOW 6 to 7 hours or on HIGH 3 to 4 hours or until chicken is tender.

2. With slotted spoon, transfer chicken to serving bowl; cover with foil to keep warm. *Turn slow cooker to HIGH.* Whisk water into cornstarch in small bowl until smooth. Stir into slow cooker. Cover; cook 15 minutes or until sauce is slightly thickened. Spoon sauce over chicken. Serve chicken over couscous; top with cilantro. Garnish with lime wedges.

# TOFU SATAY WITH PEANUT SAUCE

Makes 4 servings

## Satay

- **1 package (14 ounces) firm tofu, drained and pressed***
- ⅓ **cup water**
- ⅓ **cup soy sauce**
- **1 tablespoon dark sesame oil**
- **1 teaspoon minced garlic**
- **1 teaspoon minced fresh ginger**
- **24 white button mushrooms, trimmed**
- **1 large red bell pepper, cut into 12 pieces**

## Peanut Sauce

- **1 can (about 13 ounces) unsweetened coconut milk**
- ½ **cup creamy peanut butter**
- **2 tablespoons packed brown sugar**
- **1 tablespoon rice vinegar**
- **1 to 2 teaspoons red Thai curry paste**

*Cut tofu in half horizontally and place it between layers of paper towels. Place a weighted cutting board on top; let stand 15 to 30 minutes.*

**1.** Cut tofu into 24 cubes. Combine water, soy sauce, sesame oil, garlic and ginger in small bowl. Place tofu, mushrooms and bell pepper in large resealable food storage bag. Add soy sauce mixture; seal bag and turn gently to coat. Marinate 30 minutes, turning occasionally. Soak eight 8-inch bamboo skewers in water 20 minutes.

**2.** Preheat oven to 400°F. Spray 13×9-inch glass baking dish with nonstick cooking spray.

**3.** Drain tofu mixture; discard marinade. Thread tofu, mushrooms and bell peppers alternately on skewers. Place skewers in prepared dish.

**4.** Bake 25 minutes or until tofu cubes are lightly browned and vegetables are softened.

**5.** Meanwhile, whisk coconut milk, peanut butter, brown sugar, vinegar and curry paste in small saucepan over medium heat. Bring to a boil, stirring constantly. Reduce heat to low; cook about 20 minutes or until creamy and thick, stirring frequently. Serve satay with sauce.

# SPICY PEANUT COCONUT SHRIMP

Makes 4 servings

◇◇◇◇◇◇◇◇◇◇◇◇◇◇◇◇◇◇◇◇◇◇◇◇◇◇◇◇◇◇◇◇◇◇◇◇◇◇◇◇◇◇◇◇◇◇◇◇◇◇

¼  cup flaked coconut

2  teaspoons dark sesame oil

1  pound large raw shrimp, peeled, deveined and patted dry

¼  to ½ teaspoon red pepper flakes

2  tablespoons chopped fresh mint or cilantro (optional)

¼  cup chopped lightly salted roasted peanuts

Lime wedges (optional)

1. Toast coconut in large nonstick skillet over medium-high heat 2 to 3 minutes or until golden, stirring constantly. Immediately remove from skillet.

2. Heat oil in same skillet over medium-high heat. Add shrimp and red pepper flakes; stir-fry 3 to 4 minutes or until shrimp are pink and opaque. Add mint, if desired; toss well.

3. Transfer to serving plates. Top each serving with 1 tablespoon toasted coconut and 1 tablespoon chopped peanuts. Garnish with lime wedges.

Serving Suggestion: Serve with steamed sugar snap peas and whole wheat couscous.

# VEGETARIAN RICE NOODLES

## Makes 4 servings

〰〰〰〰〰〰〰〰〰〰〰〰〰〰〰〰〰〰〰〰

½ cup soy sauce

⅓ cup sugar

¼ cup lime juice

2 fresh red Thai chiles *or* 1 large jalapeño pepper, finely chopped

8 ounces thin rice noodles (rice vermicelli)

¼ cup coconut oil

8 ounces firm tofu, drained and cut into triangles

1 jicama (8 ounces), peeled and chopped *or* 1 can (8 ounces) sliced water chestnuts, drained

2 medium sweet potatoes (1 pound), peeled and cut into ¼-inch-thick slices

2 large leeks, cut into ¼-inch-thick slices

¼ cup chopped dry-roasted peanuts

2 tablespoons chopped fresh mint

2 tablespoons chopped fresh cilantro

1. Combine soy sauce, sugar, lime juice and chiles in small bowl until well blended; set aside.

2. Place rice noodles in medium bowl. Cover with hot water; let stand 15 minutes or until soft. Drain well; cut into 3-inch lengths.

3. Meanwhile, heat oil in large skillet over medium-high heat. Add tofu; stir-fry 4 minutes per side or until golden brown. Remove with slotted spatula to paper towel-lined baking sheet.

4. Add jicama to skillet; stir-fry 5 minutes or until lightly browned. Remove to baking sheet. Stir-fry sweet potatoes in batches until tender and browned; remove to baking sheet. Add leeks; stir-fry 1 minute.

5. Stir soy sauce mixture; add to skillet. Heat until sugar dissolves. Add noodles; toss to coat. Gently stir in tofu, vegetables, peanuts, mint and cilantro.

# COCONUT–MACADAMIA SHRIMP

Makes 6 to 8 servings

1 **pound large raw shrimp, peeled and deveined (with tails on)**

1½ **teaspoons salt, divided**

**Ground red pepper**

½ **cup all-purpose flour**

¼ **teaspoon white pepper**

1 **cup flaked coconut**

⅔ **cup panko bread crumbs**

½ **cup finely chopped macadamia nuts**

2 **eggs**

¼ **cup wheat beer**

1 **cup peanut oil**

**Apricot or pineapple preserves**

1. Spread shrimp on paper towels and pat dry. Season with ½ teaspoon salt and red pepper.

2. Combine flour, remaining 1 teaspoon salt and white pepper in shallow dish. Combine coconut, panko and macadamia nuts in another shallow dish. Whisk eggs and beer in small bowl.

3. Heat oil in deep heavy saucepan over medium-high heat to 350°F.

4. Working in small batches, dredge shrimp in flour mixture. Dip in egg mixture and roll in coconut mixture. Place carefully in oil; fry 2 minutes per side. Drain on paper towels.

5. Serve immediately with preserves for dipping.

# TOFU, VEGETABLE AND CURRY STIR-FRY

Makes 4 servings

1 package (about 14 ounces) extra-firm tofu, cut into ¾-inch cubes

¾ cup unsweetened canned coconut milk

2 tablespoons fresh lime juice

1 tablespoon curry powder

1 teaspoon dark sesame oil

2 teaspoons coconut oil, divided

4 cups broccoli florets (1½ inch pieces)

2 medium red bell peppers, cut into short, thin strips

1 medium red onion, cut into thin wedges

¼ teaspoon salt

Hot cooked brown rice (optional)

1. Press tofu cubes between layers of paper towels to remove excess moisture. Combine coconut milk, lime juice, curry powder and sesame oil in medium bowl.

2. Heat 1 teaspoon coconut oil in large nonstick skillet over medium heat. Add tofu; cook 10 minutes or until lightly browned on all sides, turning cubes often. Remove to plate; set aside.

3. Add remaining 1 teaspoon coconut oil to skillet; increase heat to high. Add broccoli, bell pepper and onion; stir-fry about 5 minutes or until vegetables are crisp-tender. Stir in tofu and coconut milk mixture; cook and stir until mixture comes to a boil. Stir in salt. Serve immediately with rice, if desired.

# SIDES & SOUPS

## AMBROSIA

Makes 4 servings

◇◇◇◇◇◇◇◇◇◇◇◇◇◇◇

**PREP TIME:** 15 minutes

1 can (20 oz.) DOLE®
   Pineapple Chunks,
   drained

1 can (11 OR 15 oz.)
   DOLE® Mandarin
   Oranges, drained

1 DOLE® Banana, sliced

1½ cups seedless grapes

½ cup miniature
   marshmallows

1 cup vanilla low-fat
   yogurt

¼ cup flaked coconut,
   toasted

• **COMBINE** pineapple chunks, mandarin oranges, banana, grapes and marshmallows in medium bowl.

• **STIR** yogurt into fruit mixture. Sprinkle with coconut.

# CHICKPEA AND ORANGE SQUASH STEW

Makes 2 servings

◇◇◇◇◇◇◇◇◇◇◇◇◇◇◇◇◇◇◇◇◇◇◇◇◇◇◇◇◇◇◇

- 1 teaspoon coconut oil
- ¾ cup chopped onion
- ½ to 1 jalapeño pepper, seeded and minced
- 1 (½-inch) piece fresh ginger, peeled and minced
- 1 clove garlic, minced
- 2 teaspoons ground cumin
- ½ teaspoon ground coriander
- 1 cup cubed peeled butternut squash, sweet potato or pumpkin
- 1 cup canned chickpeas, rinsed and drained
- ½ cup water
- 2 teaspoons soy sauce
- 1 cup unsweetened canned coconut milk

  Juice of 1 lime
- ¼ cup chopped fresh cilantro

  Spinach leaves (optional)

1. Heat oil in medium saucepan over medium-low heat. Add onion, jalapeño pepper, ginger and garlic; cook and stir 2 to 3 minutes or until onion is translucent. Add cumin and coriander; cook and stir 1 minute.

2. Add squash, chickpeas, water and soy sauce to saucepan. Bring to a boil. Reduce heat; simmer 15 minutes or until squash is tender. Add coconut milk; cook and stir 2 to 3 minutes or until heated through. Stir in lime juice and cilantro. Garnish with spinach.

# COCONUT–LIME SWEET POTATOES WITH WALNUTS

## Makes 8 servings

◇◇◇◇◇◇◇◇◇◇◇◇◇◇◇◇◇◇◇◇◇◇◇◇◇◇◇◇◇◇◇◇◇◇◇◇◇◇◇◇◇◇

2½ **pounds sweet potatoes, cut into 1-inch pieces**

8 **ounces shredded carrots**

¾ **cup flaked coconut, toasted, divided***

1 **tablespoon coconut oil or butter, melted**

3 **tablespoons sugar**

½ **teaspoon salt**

3 **tablespoons walnuts, toasted and coarsely chopped****

2 **teaspoons grated lime peel**

*To toast coconut, spread in single layer in heavy-bottomed skillet. Cook and stir over medium heat 2 to 3 minutes or until lightly browned. Remove from skillet; cool completely.*

**To toast walnuts, spread in single layer in small skillet. Cook and stir over medium heat 1 to 2 minutes or until nuts are lightly browned.*

## Slow Cooker Directions

1. Combine potatoes, carrots, ½ cup coconut, oil, sugar and salt in slow cooker. Cover; cook on LOW 5 to 6 hours. Remove to large bowl.

2. Mash potatoes with potato masher. Stir in walnuts and lime peel. Sprinkle with remaining ¼ cup coconut.

# COCONUT CURRY CHICKEN SOUP

Makes 4 servings

3 cups chicken broth

8 boneless skinless chicken thighs

1 cup chopped onion, divided

1 teaspoon salt, divided

4 whole cloves

1 tablespoon coconut oil or butter

2 tablespoons curry powder

1¼ cups unsweetened canned coconut milk

¼ cup plus 1 tablespoon chopped fresh mint, divided

3 tablespoons crystallized ginger

¼ teaspoon ground cloves

1½ cups half-and-half

1 cup cooked rice

Lime wedges (optional)

**1.** Bring broth to a boil in large skillet over high heat. Add chicken, ½ cup onion, ½ teaspoon salt and whole cloves. Return to a boil. Reduce heat; cover tightly and simmer 40 minutes or until very tender.

**2.** Remove chicken; set aside. Reserve 1 cup cooking liquid; discard remaining liquid, onion and cloves.

**3.** Increase heat to medium-high; melt oil in skillet. Add remaining ½ cup onion; cook and stir 4 minutes or until onion is translucent. Sprinkle curry powder over onion; cook 20 seconds or just until fragrant, stirring constantly.

**4.** Add coconut milk, 1 tablespoon mint, ginger, ground cloves and reserved cooking liquid to skillet. Cover and simmer 10 minutes. Add chicken; cover and simmer 15 minutes.

**5.** Stir in half-and-half and remaining ½ teaspoon salt. Shred chicken slightly, pressing down with a spoon. Cook 1 minute or until heated through. Sprinkle with remaining ¼ cup mint. Spoon rice over each serving and garnish with lime wedges.

# ASIAN SWEET POTATO AND CORN STEW

Makes 6 servings

1 tablespoon coconut or vegetable oil

1 large onion, chopped

2 tablespoons minced peeled fresh ginger

½ jalapeño or serrano pepper, seeded and minced

2 cloves garlic, minced

1 cup corn

2 teaspoons curry powder

1 can (about 13 ounces) unsweetened coconut milk

1 teaspoon cornstarch

1 can (about 14 ounces) vegetable broth

1 tablespoon soy sauce

4 sweet potatoes, peeled and cut into ¾-inch cubes

Hot cooked jasmine or other long grain rice

Chopped dry-roasted peanuts, chopped green onions and/ or chopped fresh cilantro (optional)

## Slow Cooker Directions

1. Heat oil in large skillet over medium heat. Add onion, ginger, minced jalapeño pepper and garlic. Cook about 5 minutes, stirring occasionally, or until onion softens. Remove from heat and stir in corn and curry powder.

2. Whisk coconut milk and cornstarch together in slow cooker. Stir in broth and soy sauce. Add sweet potatoes, then top with corn mixture. Cover; cook on LOW 5 to 6 hours or until sweet potatoes are tender.

3. Stir gently to smooth cooking liquid without breaking up sweet potatoes (coconut milk may look curdled). Adjust seasoning. Spoon over rice in serving bowls; garnish as desired.

# CARIBBEAN CALLALOO SOUP

Makes 6 servings

◇◇◇◇◇◇◇◇◇◇◇◇◇◇◇◇◇◇◇◇◇◇◇◇◇◇◇◇◇◇◇◇◇◇◇◇◇◇◇◇◇◇◇◇

1 teaspoon coconut oil

1 large onion, chopped

4 cloves garlic, minced

12 ounces boneless skinless chicken breasts, thinly sliced crosswise

1½ pounds butternut squash, cut into ½-inch cubes

3 cans (about 14 ounces each) chicken broth

2 jalapeño peppers, seeded and minced

2 teaspoons dried thyme

½ (10-ounce) package fresh spinach, stemmed and torn

¼ cup plus 2 tablespoons flaked coconut, toasted*

*To toast coconut, spread in single layer in heavy-bottomed skillet. Cook and stir over medium heat 2 to 3 minutes or until lightly browned. Remove from skillet; cool completely.*

**1.** Heat oil in large nonstick skillet over medium-low heat. Add onion and garlic; cook and stir 5 minutes or until onion is tender. Add chicken; cover and cook 5 to 7 minutes or until chicken is no longer pink in center.

**2.** Add squash, broth, jalapeño peppers and thyme; bring to a boil over medium-high heat. Reduce heat to low. Cover and simmer 15 to 20 minutes or until squash is very tender.

**3.** Remove from heat; stir in spinach until wilted. Ladle into bowls and sprinkle with toasted coconut.

# COOKIES & BARS

## MYSTICAL LAYERED BARS

Makes 2 to 3 dozen bars

⟨⟩⟨⟩⟨⟩⟨⟩⟨⟩⟨⟩⟨⟩⟨⟩⟨⟩⟨⟩⟨⟩⟨⟩⟨⟩⟨⟩⟨⟩⟨⟩⟨⟩⟨⟩⟨⟩⟨⟩⟨⟩⟨⟩⟨⟩

⅓ **cup (⅔ stick) butter**

1 **cup graham cracker crumbs**

½ **cup old-fashioned or quick oats**

1 **can (14 ounces) sweetened condensed milk**

1 **cup flaked coconut**

¾ **cup semisweet chocolate chips**

¾ **cup raisins**

1 **cup coarsely chopped pecans**

**1.** Preheat oven to 350°F. Melt butter in 13×9-inch baking pan. Remove from oven.

**2.** Sprinkle graham cracker crumbs and oats evenly over butter; press onto pan for form crust. Pour sweetened condensed milk evenly over crust. Layer coconut, chocolate chips, raisins and pecans over milk.

**3.** Bake 25 to 30 minutes or until lightly browned. Cool in pan on wire rack 5 minutes; cut into 2×1½-inch bars. Cool completely in pan on wire rack. Store tightly covered at room temperature or freeze up to 3 months.

# COCONUT RASPBERRY BARS

### Makes 2 to 3 dozen bars

2 cups graham cracker crumbs

½ cup (1 stick) butter, melted

1⅓ cups flaked coconut

1 can (14 ounces) sweetened condensed milk

1 cup red raspberry jam or preserves

½ cup chopped pecans

½ cup semisweet chocolate chips

½ cup white chocolate chips

1. Preheat oven to 350°F.

2. Combine graham cracker crumbs and butter in medium bowl. Press evenly onto bottom of ungreased 13×9-inch baking pan. Sprinkle with coconut; pour sweetened condensed milk evenly over coconut.

3. Bake 20 to 25 minutes or until lightly browned; cool completely in pan on wire rack.

4. Spread jam over coconut layer; sprinkle with pecans. Refrigerate for 3 to 4 hours.

5. Place semisweet chocolate chips in small resealable food storage bag; seal bag. Microwave on HIGH 1 minute. Turn bag over; heat on HIGH at 30-second intervals or until chocolate is melted. Knead bag until chocolate is smooth. Cut off very tiny corner of bag; drizzle chocolate onto jam layer. Melt white chocolate chips as directed for chocolate chips. Drizzle over top of chocolate layer; chill until chocolate is set. Cut into bars.

# PEACHY OATMEAL BARS

Makes 2 to 3 dozen bars

## Crumb Mixture

- 1½ **cups all-purpose flour**
- 1 **cup old-fashioned oats**
- ¾ **cup (1½ sticks) butter, melted**
- ½ **cup sugar**
- 2 **teaspoons almond extract**
- ½ **teaspoon baking soda**
- ¼ **teaspoon salt**

## Filling

- ¾ **cup peach preserves**
- ⅓ **cup flaked coconut**

1. Preheat oven to 350°F. Grease 9-inch square baking pan.

2. Combine flour, oats, butter, sugar, almond extract, baking soda and salt in large bowl. Beat with electric mixer at low speed 1 to 2 minutes until mixture is crumbly. Reserve ¾ cup crumb mixture; press remaining crumb mixture onto bottom of prepared baking pan.

3. Spread peach preserves to within ½ inch of edge of crumb mixture; sprinkle reserved crumb mixture and coconut over top. Bake 22 to 27 minutes or until edges are lightly browned. Cool completely. Cut into bars.

# SWEET POTATO COCONUT BARS

## Makes 2 to 3 dozen bars

30 vanilla wafers, crushed

1½ cups finely chopped walnuts, toasted, divided

1 cup flaked coconut, divided

¼ cup (½ stick) butter, softened

2 cans (15 ounces each) sweet potatoes, well drained and mashed (2 cups)

2 eggs

1 teaspoon ground cinnamon

½ teaspoon ground ginger

¼ to ½ teaspoon ground cloves

¼ teaspoon salt

1 can (14 ounces) sweetened condensed milk

1 cup butterscotch chips

1. Preheat oven to 350°F.

2. For crust, combine vanilla wafers, 1 cup walnuts, ½ cup coconut and butter in medium bowl until well blended. (Mixture will be dry and crumbly.) Press two thirds of crumb mixture onto bottom of 13×9-inch baking pan to form even layer.

3. For filling, beat mashed sweet potatoes, eggs, cinnamon, ginger, cloves and salt in large bowl with electric mixer at medium-low speed until well blended. Gradually add sweetened condensed milk; beat until well blended. Spoon filling evenly over crust. Top with remaining crumb mixture, pressing lightly into sweet potato layer.

4. Bake 25 to 30 minutes or until knife inserted into center comes out clean. Sprinkle with butterscotch chips, remaining ½ cup walnuts and ½ cup coconut. Bake 2 minutes. Cool completely in pan on wire rack. Cover and refrigerate 2 hours before serving.

# CHOCOLATE COCONUT ALMOND MACAROONS

Makes 1½ dozen cookies

◇◇◇◇◇◇◇◇◇◇◇◇◇◇◇◇◇◇◇◇◇◇◇◇◇◇◇◇◇◇◇◇◇◇◇◇◇

1⅓ **cups flaked coconut**

⅔ **cup sugar**

2 **egg whites**

½ **teaspoon vanilla**

¼ **teaspoon almond extract**

**Pinch salt**

4 **ounces sliced almonds, coarsely crushed**

18 **whole almonds**

**Chocolate Ganache (recipe follows)**

1. Combine coconut, sugar, egg whites, vanilla, almond extract and salt in medium bowl; mix well. Fold in sliced almonds. Cover and refrigerate at least 1 hour or overnight.

2. Preheat oven to 350°F. Line cookie sheet with parchment paper.

3. Shape tablespoonfuls of dough into balls. Place 1 inch apart on prepared cookie sheet. Press 1 whole almond on top of each cookie.

4. Bake 15 minutes or until light brown. Cool on cookie sheet 5 minutes. Remove to wire rack; cool completely.

5. Meanwhile, prepare Chocolate Ganache.

6. Dip bottom of each cookie into ganache. Place cookies onto clean parchment or waxed paper-lined cookie sheet. Refrigerate until ganache is set. Store covered in refrigerator.

Chocolate Ganache: Place ½ cup semisweet chocolate chips in shallow bowl. Heat ¼ cup whipping cream in small saucepan until bubbles form around edge. Pour cream over chocolate; let stand 5 minutes. Stir until smooth. Let cool 10 to 15 minutes.

# FUDGEY COCONUT CLUSTERS

Makes about 30 cookies

⬦⬦⬦⬦⬦⬦⬦⬦⬦⬦⬦⬦⬦⬦⬦⬦⬦⬦⬦⬦⬦⬦⬦⬦⬦⬦⬦⬦⬦⬦⬦⬦⬦⬦⬦⬦⬦⬦⬦⬦⬦⬦⬦⬦⬦⬦

5⅓ cups MOUNDS® Sweetened Coconut Flakes

1 can (14 ounces) sweetened condensed milk (not evaporated milk)

⅔ cup HERSHEY'S® Cocoa

¼ cup (½ stick) butter or margarine, melted

2 teaspoons vanilla extract

1½ teaspoons almond extract

HERSHEY'S® MINI KISSES® BRAND Milk Chocolates or candied cherry halves (optional)

1. Heat oven to 350°F. Line cookie sheets with parchment paper or aluminum foil greased with vegetable shortening.

2. Combine coconut, sweetened condensed milk, cocoa, melted butter, vanilla and almond extract in large bowl; mix well. Drop by rounded tablespoons onto prepared cookie sheets.

3. Bake 9 to 11 minutes or just until set; press 3 milk chocolates or candied cherry halves in center of each cookie, if desired. Immediately remove cookies to wire racks and cool completely.

Chocolate Chip Macaroons: Omit cocoa and melted butter; stir together other ingredients. Add 1 cup HERSHEY'S® Mini Chips Semi-Sweet Chocolate. Bake 9 to 11 minutes or just until set. Immediately remove to wire racks and cool completely.

# FRUITY COCONUT OATMEAL COOKIES

Makes about 3 dozen cookies

2 cups old-fashioned oats

1⅓ cups all-purpose flour

¾ teaspoon baking soda

½ teaspoon baking powder

½ teaspoon salt

¼ teaspoon ground cinnamon

1 cup packed brown sugar

¾ cup (1½ sticks) butter, softened

¼ cup granulated sugar

1 egg

1 tablespoon honey

1 teaspoon vanilla

½ cup finely diced dried mangoes

½ cup finely diced dried apples

½ cup finely diced dried cherries

3 cups flaked coconut, divided

1. Preheat oven to 350°F. Line cookie sheets with parchment paper. Combine oats, flour, baking soda, baking powder, salt and cinnamon in medium bowl.

2. Beat brown sugar, butter and granulated sugar in large bowl with electric mixer at medium speed until light and fluffy. Add egg, honey and vanilla; beat until well blended. Gradually add flour mixture; beat just until blended. Stir in mangoes, apples, cherries and ½ cup coconut.

3. Spread remaining 2½ cups coconut in shallow bowl. Drop dough by rounded tablespoonfuls into coconut and roll to coat; place on prepared cookie sheets.

4. Bake 15 to 17 minutes or until puffed and golden. Cool 5 minutes on cookie sheets. Remove to wire racks; cool completely.

Variation: Substitute 1 package (6 ounces) of tropical medley dried chopped fruit for the mangoes, apples and cherries.

# CRANBERRY COCONUT BARS

Makes 12 to 16 bars

## Filling

1½  cups sweetened
     dried cranberries or
     cherries
½  cup flaked coconut
⅔  cup half-and-half
1  teaspoon vanilla

## Crust

2  cups quick-cooking
   oats
1  cup packed dark
   brown sugar
¾  cup all-purpose flour
½  teaspoon baking soda
½  teaspoon ground
   cinnamon
½  cup (1 stick) butter,
   melted

1. For filling, heat cranberries, coconut and half-and-half in medium saucepan over medium heat. Cook 10 to 12 minutes or until mixture boils and thickens, stirring occasionally. Remove from heat; stir in vanilla. Cool in saucepan.

2. For crust, combine oats, brown sugar, flour, baking soda and cinnamon in medium bowl; mix well. Add melted butter; stir until moist and crumbly. Firmly press about two thirds of crust mixture into bottom of ungreased 8-inch square baking pan. Refrigerate 30 to 60 minutes or until firm.

3. Preheat oven to 350°F. Spread cooled filling evenly over crust. Sprinkle remaining crust mixture over filling; press gently into filling.

4. Bake 25 to 30 minutes or until topping is crisp and lightly browned. Cool completely in pan on wire rack. Cut into bars.

Tip: You can turn old-fashioned oats into quick-cooking oats by pulsing them in a food processor or blender.

# CHOCOLATE MACAROON BARS

Makes about 24 bars

◇◇◇◇◇◇◇◇◇◇◇◇◇◇◇◇◇◇◇◇◇◇◇◇◇◇◇◇◇◇◇◇◇◇◇◇◇◇◇◇◇◇◇◇◇◇

1¼ cups graham cracker crumbs

⅓ cup sugar

¼ cup HERSHEY'S® Cocoa

⅓ cup butter or margarine, melted

1 can (14 ounces) sweetened condensed milk (not evaporated milk)

2⅔ cups MOUNDS® Sweetened Coconut Flakes

2 cups fresh white bread crumbs (about 5 slices)

2 eggs

2 teaspoons vanilla extract

1 cup HERSHEY'S® Mini Chips Semi-Sweet Chocolate

1. Heat oven to 350°F.

2. Stir together graham cracker crumbs, sugar, cocoa and butter in large bowl; press firmly onto bottom of ungreased 13×9×2-inch baking pan.

3. Bake 10 minutes. Meanwhile, combine sweetened condensed milk, coconut, bread crumbs, eggs, vanilla and small chocolate chips in large bowl; stir until blended. Spoon over prepared crust, spreading evenly.

4. Bake 30 minutes or until lightly browned. Cool completely in pan on wire rack. Cut into bars. Store covered in refrigerator.

# LEMON ICED AMBROSIA BARS

## Makes 2 to 3 dozen bars

1¾ cups all-purpose flour, divided

2⅓ cups powdered sugar, divided

¾ cup (1½ sticks) cold butter

2 cups packed brown sugar

4 eggs, beaten

1 cup flaked coconut

1 cup finely chopped pecans

½ teaspoon baking powder

3 tablespoons lemon juice

2 tablespoons softened butter

1. Preheat oven to 350°F. Lightly grease 13×9-inch baking pan.

2. Combine 1½ cups flour and ⅓ cup powdered sugar in medium bowl; cut in cold butter with pastry blender or two knives until mixture resembles coarse crumbs. Press onto bottom of prepared pan; bake 15 minutes.

3. Meanwhile, combine remaining ¼ cup flour, brown sugar, eggs, coconut, pecans and baking powder in medium bowl; mix well. Spread evenly over baked crust; bake 20 minutes. Cool completely in pan on wire rack.

4. Stir together remaining 2 cups powdered sugar, lemon juice and softened butter in small bowl until smooth. Spread over bars. Cover and refrigerate until cold. Cut into bars. Store leftovers covered in refrigerator.

# CHOCOLATE CHIP COCONUT COOKIES

Makes about 3 dozen cookies

⬦⬦⬦⬦⬦⬦⬦⬦⬦⬦⬦⬦⬦⬦⬦⬦⬦⬦⬦⬦⬦⬦⬦⬦

⅔ cup butter or margarine, softened

1 cup sugar

2 eggs

½ teaspoon vanilla extract

¼ to ½ teaspoon almond extract

2 cups all-purpose flour

1 teaspoon baking powder

1 teaspoon salt

½ teaspoon baking soda

½ cup dairy sour cream

2 cups MOUNDS® Sweetened Coconut Flakes

2 cups (12-ounce package) HERSHEY'S® Mini Chips Semi-Sweet Chocolate

Additional sugar

Sliced almonds

1. Heat oven to 350°F. Lightly grease cookie sheets or line with parchment paper.

2. Beat butter and sugar in large bowl until creamy. Add eggs, vanilla and almond extract, beating until light and fluffy. Stir together flour, baking powder, salt and baking soda; add to butter mixture alternately with sour cream, beating until well blended. Stir in coconut and small chocolate chips. Drop dough by tablespoons onto prepared cookie sheet. Sprinkle with sugar; top with almonds.

3. Bake 15 to 18 minutes or until edges are lightly browned. Remove from cookie sheet to wire rack. Cool completely.

# CHOCOLATE-COCONUT-TOFFEE DELIGHTS

### Makes 1 dozen large cookies

½ cup all-purpose flour

¼ teaspoon baking powder

¼ teaspoon salt

1 package (12 ounces) semisweet chocolate chips, divided

¼ cup (½ stick) butter, cut into small pieces

¾ cup packed brown sugar

2 eggs, beaten

1 teaspoon vanilla

1½ cups flaked coconut

1 cup toffee baking bits

½ cup bittersweet chocolate chips

1. Preheat oven to 350°F. Line cookie sheets with parchment paper. Combine flour, baking powder and salt in small bowl.

2. Place 1 cup semisweet chocolate chips and butter in large microwavable bowl. Microwave on HIGH 1 minute; stir. Microwave at additional 30-second intervals, stirring after each interval, until mixture is melted and smooth.

3. Beat brown sugar, eggs and vanilla with electric mixer at medium speed. Beat in chocolate mixture until well blended. Add flour mixture; beat at low speed until blended. Stir in coconut, toffee bits and remaining 1 cup semisweet chocolate chips. Drop dough by heaping ⅓ cupfuls 3 inches apart onto prepared cookie sheets. Flatten with rubber spatula into 3½-inch circles.

4. Bake 15 to 17 minutes or until edges are firm to the touch. Cool on cookie sheets 2 minutes; slide parchment paper and cookies onto wire racks. Cool completely.

5. For chocolate drizzle, place bittersweet chocolate chips in small microwavable bowl. Microwave on HIGH 30 seconds; stir. Microwave at additional 30-second intervals, stirring after each interval, until melted and smooth. Drizzle over cookies. Let stand until set.

# CAKES & CUPCAKES

## COCONUT PINEAPPLE POKE CAKE

Makes 12 to 16 servings

◇◇◇◇◇◇◇◇◇◇◇◇◇◇◇◇◇◇◇◇◇◇◇◇◇◇◇◇◇◇◇◇◇◇◇◇◇◇◇◇◇◇◇◇◇◇

1 package (about 15 ounces) white cake mix, plus ingredients to prepare mix

1 can (20 ounces) crushed pineapple, ¼ cup juice reserved

1 can (14 ounces) sweetened condensed milk

1 package (14 ounces each) flaked coconut, toasted,* divided

1 cup chopped maraschino cherries, drained

*To toast coconut, spread evenly on ungreased cookie sheet. Toast in preheated 350°F oven 5 to 7 minutes, stirring occasionally, until light golden brown.*

1. Prepare and bake cake mix according to package directions for 13×9-inch pan. Cool completely.

2. Combine pineapple, sweetened condensed milk and half of coconut in small bowl; mix well.

3. Poke holes in cake at ½-inch intervals using fork. Pour reserved ¼ cup pineapple juice over cake and into holes. Spread pineapple mixture over cake. Sprinkle remaining coconut and cherries over cake and into holes. Refrigerate 2 to 3 hours or until firm.

# PIÑA COLADA CAKE

Makes 12 servings

◇◇◇◇◇◇◇◇◇◇◇◇◇◇◇◇◇◇◇◇◇◇◇◇◇◇◇◇◇◇◇◇

1 package (about 15 ounces) white cake mix, plus ingredients to prepare mix

2½ cup cold whipping cream

¼ cup dark rum

¾ cup plus 2 tablespoons powdered sugar, divided

2¾ teaspoons vanilla, divided

1 fresh pineapple, peeled, cut in half lengthwise and cored

2 cups flaked coconut, toasted*

*To toast coconut, spread evenly on ungreased cookie sheet. Toast in preheated 350°F oven 5 to 7 minutes, stirring occasionally, until light golden brown.

1. Prepare cake mix and bake according to package directions for two (9-inch) round cake pans. Cool in pans on wire racks 15 minutes. Remove cakes from pans; cool completely.

2. For filling, combine ½ cup cream, rum, 2 tablespoons powdered sugar and ¾ teaspoon vanilla until well blended. Cover with plastic wrap; refrigerate until ready to use.

3. For topping, beat remaining 2 cups whipping cream in large bowl with electric mixer at high speed 1½ to 2 minutes or until soft peaks form. Add remaining ¾ cup powdered sugar and 2 teaspoons vanilla; beat 20 seconds or until stiff peaks form. Cover with plastic wrap; refrigerate until ready to use.

4. Place pineapple cut side down on cutting board; slice very thinly. Place slices on paper towels; pat dry.

5. Place one cake layer on serving plate. Spread half of filling evenly over cake. Spread 1 cup topping evenly over cake. Sprinkle with 1 cup coconut; top with remaining cake layer. Spread remaining filling evenly over cake. Spread remaining topping evenly over top and side of cake; sprinkle top with remaining coconut.

6. Press pineapple slices around side of cake vertically, overlapping slightly. Reserve any remaining pineapple slices for another use. Refrigerate cake until ready to serve.

# GERMAN CHOCOLATE CUPCAKES

Makes 22 cupcakes

◇◇◇◇◇◇◇◇◇◇◇◇◇◇◇◇◇◇◇◇◇◇◇◇◇◇◇◇◇◇◇◇◇◇◇◇◇◇◇◇◇◇◇◇◇◇◇◇◇◇

1 package (about 16 ounces) German chocolate cake mix, plus ingredients to prepare mix

1 can (12 ounces) evaporated milk

¾ cup granulated sugar

½ cup (1 stick) butter, softened

4 egg yolks

¼ cup packed brown sugar

2 cups flaked coconut

1 cup chopped pecans

3 ounces semisweet chocolate, finely chopped

1. Preheat oven to 350°F. Line 22 standard (2½-inch) muffin cups with paper baking cups.

2. Prepare cake mix according to package directions. Spoon batter evenly into prepared muffin cups. Bake 20 minutes or until toothpick inserted into centers comes out clean. Cool in pans 10 minutes. Remove to wire racks; cool completely.

3. Combine evaporated milk, granulated sugar, butter, egg yolks and brown sugar in medium saucepan; whisk until blended. Cook over medium-low heat 8 to 10 minutes or until slightly thickened and mixture just begins to bubble, stirring constantly. Stir in coconut and pecans. Remove from heat; let stand 1 hour or until thickened, stirring occasionally.

4. Spoon cooled coconut mixture evenly over each cupcake.

5. Microwave chocolate in small microwavable bowl on HIGH 30 seconds; stir. Microwave at additional 15-second intervals until chocolate is melted. Drizzle over cupcakes; let stand until set.

# DARK CHOCOLATE COCONUT CAKE

### Makes 12 to 16 servings

◇◇◇◇◇◇◇◇◇◇◇◇◇◇◇◇◇◇◇◇◇◇◇◇◇◇◇◇◇◇◇◇◇◇◇◇◇◇◇◇◇◇◇◇◇◇◇◇◇◇◇◇

1 **package (about 15 ounces) devil's food cake mix, plus ingredients to prepare mix**

1 **cup strong coffee**

½ **cup evaporated milk**

¼ **cup (½ stick) butter, divided**

3 **cups mini marshmallows\***

1 **package (14 ounces) flaked coconut**

1 **cup whipping cream**

2 **cups (12 ounces) semisweet chocolate chips\*\***

*\*Or substitute 24 large marshmallows.*

*\*\*For more intense chocolate flavor, use bittersweet or dark chocolate chips.*

1. Preheat oven to 350°F. Spray two 8-inch round cake pans with nonstick cooking spray. Prepare cake mix according to package directions, substituting coffee for water. Pour batter evenly into prepared pans. Bake 23 to 25 minutes or until toothpick inserted into centers comes out clean. Cool completely in pans on wire racks.

2. For filling, bring evaporated milk and 2 tablespoons butter to a boil in medium saucepan over medium heat. Add marshmallows; stir until smooth. Remove from heat; stir in coconut. Cool completely.

3. For ganache, heat cream and remaining 2 tablespoons butter in medium saucepan over medium-low heat. (Do not boil.) Remove from heat; add chocolate chips. Let stand 1 minute; stir until smooth.

4. Cut each cake layer in half horizontally. Place one cake layer on serving plate; spread with one third of filling almost to edge. Repeat layers twice. Top with remaining cake layer. Frost top and side of cake with ganache; refrigerate until set. Store leftovers in refrigerator.

# SPICY COCONUT–LIME CUPCAKES

### Makes 12 cupcakes

1¾ cups all-purpose flour

1½ teaspoons baking powder

1 teaspoon salt

½ teaspoon baking soda

½ teaspoon ground red pepper

¾ cup sugar

½ cup (1 stick) butter, softened

¾ cup unsweetened canned coconut milk, well shaken

2 eggs

¼ cup milk

Grated peel and juice of 2 limes

⅓ cup flaked coconut

Coconut-Lime Whipped Cream (recipe follows)

⅓ cup flaked coconut, toasted*

Additional grated lime peel (optional)

*To toast coconut, spread evenly on ungreased cookie sheet. Toast in preheated 350°F oven 5 to 7 minutes, stirring occasionally, until light golden brown.*

1. Preheat oven to 350°F. Line 12 standard (2½-inch) muffin cups with paper baking cups.

2. Combine flour, baking powder, salt, baking soda and ground red pepper in medium bowl. Beat sugar and butter in large bowl with electric mixer at medium speed until creamy. Add coconut milk, eggs, milk, lime peel and lime juice; beat until blended. Add flour mixture and ⅓ cup coconut; beat at low speed just until blended. Spoon batter evenly into prepared muffin cups.

3. Bake 18 to 20 minutes or until toothpick inserted into centers comes out clean. Cool cupcakes in pan 5 minutes. Remove to wire rack; cool completely.

4. Prepare Coconut-Lime Whipped Cream. Frost cupcakes; top with toasted coconut and additional lime peel, if desired. Store in refrigerator.

Coconut-Lime Whipped Cream:
Beat 1 cup whipping cream in large bowl with electric mixer at medium-high speed until soft peaks form. Add 2½ tablespoons well-shaken coconut milk, 1 tablespoon sugar and grated peel and juice of 1 lime; beat until stiff peaks form.

# INDIVIDUAL CHOCOLATE COCONUT CHEESECAKES

Makes 12 servings

1 cup chocolate cookie crumbs

¼ cup (½ stick) butter, melted

2 packages (8 ounces each) cream cheese, softened

⅓ cup sugar

2 eggs

1 teaspoon vanilla

¼ teaspoon coconut extract

½ cup flaked coconut

½ cup semisweet chocolate chips

1 teaspoon shortening

1. Preheat oven to 325°F. Line 12 standard (2½-inch) muffin cups with foil or paper baking cups.

2. Combine cookie crumbs and butter in small bowl. Press into bottoms of prepared cups.

3. Beat cream cheese and sugar in large bowl with electric mixer at medium speed 2 minutes or until well blended. Add eggs, vanilla and coconut extract; beat until blended. Stir in coconut. Carefully spoon about ¼ cup batter into each prepared baking cup.

4. Bake 18 to 22 minutes or until nearly set. Cool in pan on wire rack 30 minutes. Remove cheesecakes from pan; peel off baking cups.

5. Melt chocolate chips and shortening in small saucepan over low heat until chocolate is melted, stirring frequently. Drizzle over cheesecakes. Let stand 20 minutes. Refrigerate until ready to serve.

# GERMAN CHOCOLATE POKE CAKE

Makes 12 to 16 servings

◇◇◇◇◇◇◇◇◇◇◇◇◇◇◇◇◇◇◇◇◇◇◇◇◇◇◇◇◇◇◇◇◇◇◇◇◇◇◇◇◇◇◇◇◇

1  package (about 15 ounces) German chocolate cake mix, plus ingredients to prepare mix

1  jar (12 ounces) caramel ice cream topping

1  can (12 ounces) evaporated milk

¾  cup granulated sugar

¾  cup packed brown sugar

½  cup (1 stick) butter, softened

4  egg yolks, beaten

2  cups flaked coconut

1  cup chopped pecans

1. Prepare and bake cake mix according to package directions for 13×9-inch pan. Cool completely.

2. Poke holes in cake at ½-inch intervals with wooden skewer. Microwave caramel in jar without lid on HIGH 1 to 2 minutes or until softened; stir. Pour over cake.

3. Combine evaporated milk, granulated sugar, brown sugar, butter and egg yolks in medium saucepan; cook and stir over medium-low heat 8 to 10 minutes or until slightly thickened and mixture just begins to bubble. Stir in coconut and pecans. Remove from heat. Pour coconut mixture over cake. Refrigerate 2 to 3 hours or until firm.

# COCONUT CREAM POKE CAKE

## Makes 12 to 16 servings

◇◇◇◇◇◇◇◇◇◇◇◇◇◇◇◇◇◇◇◇◇◇◇◇◇◇◇◇◇◇◇◇◇◇◇◇◇◇◇◇◇◇◇◇◇

1 package (about 15 ounces) yellow cake mix, plus ingredients to prepare mix

1 package (4-serving size) coconut cream instant pudding and pie filling mix, plus ingredients to prepare mix

1½ cups sweetened flaked coconut, toasted*

*To toast coconut, spread evenly on ungreased cookie sheet. Toast in preheated 350°F oven 5 to 7 minutes, stirring occasionally, until light golden brown.*

1. Prepare and bake cake mix according to package directions for 13×9-inch pan. Cool completely.

2. Prepare pudding mix according to package directions. Poke cake at ½-inch intervals. Pour pudding over top of cake. Sprinkle with toasted coconut.

# TROPICAL ANGEL FOOD CAKE

Makes 8 servings

◇◇◇◇◇◇◇◇◇◇◇◇◇◇◇◇◇◇◇◇◇◇◇◇◇◇◇◇◇◇◇◇◇◇◇◇◇◇◇◇◇◇◇◇◇◇

1   prepared angel food cake

1   container (8 ounces) whipped topping, thawed

1   can (8 ounces) crushed pineapple with juice

1   package (4-serving size) vanilla instant pudding and pie filling mix

1   ripe banana, thinly sliced

1   cup flaked coconut, toasted*

4   slices fresh or canned pineapple, cut in half

*To toast coconut, spread in single layer in heavy-bottomed skillet. Cook and stir over medium heat 2 to 3 minutes or until lightly browned. Remove from skillet; cool completely.

1. Cut cake horizontally into three even layers. Combine whipped topping, crushed pineapple and pudding mix in large bowl; mix well.

2. Arrange half of banana slices on bottom cake layer. Spread with ¾ cup whipped topping mixture. Top with middle layer of cake. Layer with remaining banana slices, ¾ cup topping mixture and top cake later. Frost top and sides of cake with remaining topping mixture. Press coconut onto side of cake. Arrange pineapple slices on top of cake.

Variation: Add sliced strawberries and/or kiwi as garnish or between cake layers.

# COCONUT CAKE

## Makes 10 to 12 servings

◇◇◇◇◇◇◇◇◇◇◇◇◇◇◇◇◇◇◇◇◇◇◇◇◇◇◇◇

1 package (about 15 ounces) white cake mix

1 can (about 13 ounces) unsweetened coconut milk

4 egg whites

1 container (16 ounces) vanilla frosting

2 cups flaked coconut

1. Preheat oven to 350°F. Spray two 8-inch round cake pans with nonstick cooking spray; line bottoms with parchment paper.

2. Beat cake mix, coconut milk and egg whites in large bowl with electric mixer at low speed 30 seconds. Beat at medium-low speed 2 minutes or until well blended. Divide batter evenly between prepared pans.

3. Bake about 30 minutes or until toothpick inserted into centers comes out clean. Cool in pans 10 minutes. Remove to wire racks; cool completely.

4. Place one cake layer on serving plate; spread with vanilla frosting. Top with remaining layer; frost side and top of cake with remaining frosting.

5. Press coconut into frosting on top and side of cake.

# CREAMY COCONUT CAKE WITH ALMOND FILLING

### Makes 10 to 12 servings

1 package (about 15 ounces) white cake mix

1 cup sour cream

3 eggs

½ cup vegetable oil

1 teaspoon vanilla

1 teaspoon coconut extract

1 can (12½ ounces) almond filling

2 containers (16 ounces each) creamy coconut frosting

½ cup sliced almonds

1. Preheat oven to 350°F. Grease and flour two 9-inch round baking pans. Tap pans to remove excess flour.

2. Beat cake mix, sour cream, eggs, oil, vanilla and coconut extract in large bowl with electric mixer at low speed 3 minutes or until well blended. Divide batter evenly between prepared pans.

3. Bake about 30 minutes or until toothpicks inserted into centers come out clean. Cool completely in pans on wire racks.

4. Remove cake layers from pans; cut each layer in half horizontally. Place one cake layer on serving plate; spread with half of almond filling. Top with second cake layer; spread with ½ cup coconut frosting. Top with third cake layer; spread with remaining almond filling. Top with fourth cake layer; spread remaining coconut frosting over top and side of cake. Sprinkle with almonds.

# PIES & COBBLERS

## CLASSIC COCONUT PIE

Makes 8 servings

◇◇◇◇◇◇◇◇◇◇◇◇◇◇◇◇◇◇◇◇◇◇◇◇◇◇◇◇◇◇◇◇◇◇◇◇◇◇◇◇

1¼ **cups sugar, divided**

½ **cup self-rising flour**

1¼ **cups milk**

3 **eggs, separated**

2 **tablespoons butter**

1 **teaspoon vanilla**

1¼ **cups flaked coconut, divided**

1 **baked 9-inch pie crust**

**1.** Preheat oven to 350°F.

**2.** Combine 1 cup sugar and flour in medium saucepan; mix well. Whisk in milk, egg yolks, butter and vanilla until well blended; cook over medium heat until mixture thickens, whisking constantly. Remove from heat; stir in 1 cup coconut. Pour into baked crust.

**3.** Beat egg whites in large bowl with electric mixer at high speed until foamy. Gradually add remaining ¼ cup sugar, beating until soft peaks form. Spread meringue over filling. Sprinkle with remaining ¼ cup coconut.

**4.** Bake 10 to 15 minutes or until coconut is golden brown. Cool completely on wire rack.

# TROPICAL FRUIT COBBLER

Makes 8 servings

⬦⬦⬦⬦⬦⬦⬦⬦⬦⬦⬦⬦⬦⬦⬦⬦⬦⬦⬦⬦⬦⬦⬦⬦⬦⬦⬦⬦⬦⬦⬦⬦⬦⬦⬦⬦⬦⬦

⅔ pineapple, peeled, cored and cut into 1-inch pieces (about 4 cups)

2 mangoes, peeled, pitted and cut into 1-inch pieces (about 4 cups)

2 bananas, halved lengthwise and cut crosswise into 1-inch pieces

½ cup plus 5 tablespoons sugar, divided

2 tablespoons cornstarch

¼ teaspoon ground allspice

1 cup all-purpose flour

¼ cup flaked coconut

1 teaspoon baking powder

¼ teaspoon salt

¼ cup (½ stick) cold butter, cut into small pieces

½ cup plus 2 tablespoons whipping cream, divided

½ teaspoon coconut extract

1. Preheat oven to 375°F. Spray 2-quart oval baking dish with nonstick cooking spray.

2. Combine pineapple, mangoes, bananas, ½ cup sugar, cornstarch and allspice in large bowl; toss to coat. Spoon into prepared baking dish.

3. Combine flour, coconut, 3 tablespoons sugar, baking powder and salt in medium bowl; mix well. Cut in butter with pastry blender or two knives until mixture resembles coarse crumbs. Add ½ cup cream and coconut extract; stir until rough dough forms. Knead dough several times in bowl until it holds together.

4. Turn out dough onto lightly floured surface; roll into 8- to 9-inch circle about ¼ inch thick. Cut circle into 1-inch-wide strips; cut each strip on a diagonal to form 2½×1-inch diamond shapes (or cut into squares). Arrange shortbread diamonds over fruit mixture. Brush dough with remaining 2 tablespoons cream; sprinkle generously with remaining 2 tablespoons sugar.

5. Bake 45 to 47 minutes or until filling is thick and bubbly and shortbread is golden brown. Let stand 30 minutes before serving.

# COCONUT CREAM PIE BOWLS

Makes 6 servings

2 cups milk

¼ cup sugar

3 tablespoons cornstarch

⅛ teaspoon salt

1 egg

¾ cup flaked coconut

1 tablespoon butter

1 teaspoon vanilla

1 teaspoon coconut extract

¾ cup whipped cream or whipped topping

1. Combine milk, sugar, cornstarch and salt in medium saucepan. Whisk until well blended and cornstarch is dissolved. Cook over medium heat until mixture thickens and begins to boil, stirring constantly. Boil 1 minute; remove from heat.

2. Whisk 2 tablespoons milk mixture into egg in small bowl until well blended. Slowly pour mixture back into saucepan, stirring rapidly to avoid lumps. Cook over medium heat 5 minutes until mixture thickens, stirring constantly. Remove from heat.

3. Stir in coconut, butter, vanilla and coconut extract. Pour into six 6-ounce ramekins; refrigerate until firm. Top with whipped topping before serving.

# AMARETTO COCONUT CREAM PIE

Makes 8 servings

◇◇◇◇◇◇◇◇◇◇◇◇◇◇◇◇◇◇◇◇◇◇◇◇◇◇◇◇◇◇◇◇◇◇◇◇◇◇◇◇◇◇◇◇◇◇◇◇

¼   cup flaked coconut

1   container (8 ounces) whipped topping, divided

1   container (6 ounces) coconut or vanilla yogurt

¼   cup amaretto liqueur

1   package (4-serving size) coconut instant pudding and pie filling mix

1   (6-ounce) graham cracker pie crust

Fresh strawberries (optional)

1. Preheat oven to 350°F. Spread coconut in even layer on baking sheet. Bake 5 minutes or until golden brown, stirring frequently. Cool completely.

2. Combine 2 cups whipped topping, yogurt and amaretto in large bowl; stir until blended. Add pudding mix; whisk 2 minutes or until thickened.

3. Spread mixture evenly in pie crust; spread remaining whipped topping over filling. Sprinkle with toasted coconut. Garnish with strawberries. Refrigerate until ready to serve.

# CHOCOLATE COCONUT PECAN PIE

Makes 8 servings

PREP TIME: 15 minutes    BAKE TIME: 50 to 55 minutes

1   cup flaked coconut

1   cup semisweet
    chocolate chips

1   cup coarsely chopped
    pecans

1   (9-inch) unbaked
    deep-dish pie crust

⅔   cup KARO® Light or
    Dark Corn Syrup

½   cup granulated sugar

½   cup packed brown
    sugar

2   tablespoons butter or
    margarine, melted

4   eggs

1. Mix coconut, chocolate chips and pecans in a medium bowl; sprinkle over bottom of pie crust. Combine corn syrup, sugars, butter and eggs until well blended.

2. Pour over coconut mixture.

3. Bake in a preheated 350°F oven for 50 to 55 minutes or until puffed and set. Cool on wire rack.

For a Classic Pecan Pie: Mix 1 cup KARO® Light or Dark Corn Syrup, 3 eggs, 1 cup sugar, 2 tablespoons melted butter and 1 teaspoon SPICE ISLANDS® 100% Pure Bourbon Vanilla Extract in a medium bowl. Stir in 1½ cups (6 ounces) whole pecans. Pour into 1 (9-inch) unbaked deep-dish pie crust. Bake in preheated 350°F oven for 60 to 70 minutes.

Note: For any pecan pie recipe, KARO® Lite Syrup may be substituted for KARO® Corn Syrup.

# COCONUT CHERRY COBBLER FOR A CROWD

### Makes 16 servings

2 packages (12 ounces each) frozen dark sweet cherries, thawed and juice reserved

1 cup water

1 tablespoon lemon juice

2 teaspoons almond extract

2 cups sugar, divided

¼ cup cornstarch

¾ teaspoon salt, divided

3 cups all-purpose flour

1 cup toasted coconut*

1½ teaspoons baking powder

1 cup (2 sticks) butter, softened

4 eggs

*To toast coconut, spread evenly on ungreased cookie sheet. Toast in preheated 350°F oven 5 to 7 minutes, stirring occasionally, until light golden brown.*

1. Preheat oven to 350°F. Spray 15×10-inch jelly-roll pan with nonstick cooking spray.

2. Combine cherries with juice, water, lemon juice and almond extract in large saucepan. Stir in ¾ cup sugar, cornstarch and ¼ teaspoon salt; bring to a boil over medium-high heat. Cook and stir about 2 minutes or until thickened.

3. Combine flour, coconut, baking powder and remaining ½ teaspoon salt in medium bowl; mix well. Beat butter and remaining 1¼ cups sugar in large bowl with electric mixer at medium speed until light and fluffy. Add eggs; beat until well blended. Stir in flour mixture until blended.

4. Reserve 1¼ cups dough for topping. Spread remaining dough on bottom of prepared pan using damp hands. (Dough will be thick and sticky). Spread cherry mixture evenly over dough. Crumble remaining dough over cherries.

5. Bake 35 to 40 minutes or until crust is golden brown.

# BANANA-COCONUT CREAM PIE

## Makes 8 servings

### Crust

- **1 cup almonds**
- **1 tablespoon sugar**
- **½ cup flaked coconut**
- **¼ cup (½ stick) butter, cut into small pieces**
- **Pinch salt**

### Filling

- **2 bananas**
- **1 teaspoon lemon juice**
- **½ cup sugar**
- **¼ cup cornstarch**
- **¼ teaspoon salt**
- **3 cups whole milk**
- **2 egg yolks**
- **1 teaspoon vanilla**

### Topping

- **1 banana**
- **2 tablespoons flaked coconut, toasted***
- **Whipped cream**

*To toast coconut, spread evenly on ungreased cookie sheet. Toast in preheated 350°F oven 5 to 7 minutes, stirring occasionally, until light golden brown.*

**1.** Preheat oven to 350°F. Grease 9-inch pie pan.

**2.** Place almonds and 1 tablespoon sugar in food processor; process using on/off pulses until almonds are ground. Add ½ cup coconut; pulse to combine. Add butter and pinch of salt; pulse until mixture begins to stick together. Press mixture onto bottom and up side of prepared pan. Bake 10 to 12 minutes or until golden around edge. Cool completely.

**3.** Slice 2 bananas; sprinkle with lemon juice. Layer on bottom of prepared crust.

**4.** Combine ½ cup sugar, cornstarch and ¼ teaspoon salt in medium saucepan. Whisk milk and egg yolks in medium bowl until well blended; slowly stir into sugar mixture. Cook and stir over medium heat until thickened. Bring to a boil; boil 1 minute. Remove from heat; stir in vanilla.

**5.** Pour mixture over bananas in crust. Cover and refrigerate at least 2 hours or until ready to serve.

**6.** Slice remaining banana; arrange on top of pie. Sprinkle with 2 tablespoons coconut and top with whipped cream.

# CARIBBEAN COCONUT PIE

Makes 8 servings

1 unbaked 9-inch deep-dish pie crust

1 can (14 ounces) sweetened condensed milk

¾ cup flaked coconut

2 eggs

½ cup hot water

2 teaspoons grated lime peel

Juice of 1 lime

¼ teaspoon salt

⅛ teaspoon ground red pepper

Whipped cream (optional)

1. Preheat oven to 400°F. Prick holes in bottom of crust with fork. Bake 10 minutes or until lightly browned. Cool 15 minutes on wire rack.

2. *Reduce oven temperature to 350°F.* Combine sweetened condensed milk, coconut, eggs, water, lime peel, lime juice, salt and red pepper in large bowl. Pour into crust.

3. Bake 30 minutes or until knife inserted into center comes out clean. Cool completely on wire rack.

4. Serve with whipped cream, if desired. Store leftovers covered in refrigerator.

# STRAWBERRY MANGO CRISP WITH ALMOND COCONUT STREUSEL

Makes 8 servings

◇◇◇◇◇◇◇◇◇◇◇◇◇◇◇◇◇◇◇◇◇◇◇◇◇◇◇◇◇◇◇◇◇◇◇◇◇◇◇◇◇◇

2 pounds fresh strawberries, hulled and cut into ¼-inch slices

1 mango, peeled, pitted and cut into ½-inch pieces

½ cup granulated sugar

3 tablespoons cornstarch

½ cup all-purpose flour

½ cup old-fashioned oats

½ cup slivered almonds

¼ cup flaked coconut

¼ cup packed brown sugar

¼ teaspoon salt

¼ cup (½ stick) butter, cut into small pieces

1. Preheat oven to 375°F. Spray 8-inch square baking pan with nonstick cooking spray.

2. Combine strawberries, mango, granulated sugar and cornstarch in large bowl; toss to coat. Spoon into prepared pan.

3. Combine flour, oats, almonds, coconut, brown sugar and salt in medium bowl; mix well. Add butter; mix with fingertips until mixture resembles pea-sized crumbs. Sprinkle evenly over fruit mixture.

4. Bake 45 minutes or until filling is bubbly and topping is golden brown. Let stand 1 hour before serving.

# NO-BAKE COCONUT CREAM PIE

Makes 12 servings

◇◇◇◇◇◇◇◇◇◇◇◇◇◇◇◇◇◇◇◇◇◇◇◇◇◇◇◇◇◇◇◇◇◇◇◇◇◇◇◇◇◇◇◇◇◇

2  tablespoons water

1  packet (¼ ounce) unflavored gelatin

1  can (about 14 ounces) unsweetened coconut milk

1  package (8 ounces) cream cheese, softened

6  tablespoons sugar

2  teaspoons vanilla

1  teaspoon coconut extract

1  (6-ounce) graham cracker pie crust

¼  cup flaked coconut, toasted*

*To toast coconut, spread in single layer in heavy-bottomed skillet. Cook and stir over medium heat 2 to 3 minutes or until lightly browned. Remove from skillet; cool completely.

1. Place water in small microwavable bowl. Sprinkle gelatin over water; let stand 1 minute. Microwave on HIGH 20 seconds or until gelatin is completely dissolved.

2. Combine coconut milk, cream cheese, sugar, vanilla, coconut extract and gelatin mixture in blender; blend until smooth. Pour mixture into prepared crust; cover and chill about 4 hours or until firm.

3. Before serving, sprinkle toasted coconut over pie.

# ACKNOWLEDGMENTS

The publisher would like to thank the companies and organizations listed below for the use of their recipes and photographs in this publication.

**ACH Food Companies, Inc.**

**Dole Food Company, Inc.**

**The Hershey Company**

# METRIC CONVERSION CHART

## VOLUME MEASUREMENTS (dry)

$1/8$ teaspoon = 0.5 mL
$1/4$ teaspoon = 1 mL
$1/2$ teaspoon = 2 mL
$3/4$ teaspoon = 4 mL
1 teaspoon = 5 mL
1 tablespoon = 15 mL
2 tablespoons = 30 mL
$1/4$ cup = 60 mL
$1/3$ cup = 75 mL
$1/2$ cup = 125 mL
$2/3$ cup = 150 mL
$3/4$ cup = 175 mL
1 cup = 250 mL
2 cups = 1 pint = 500 mL
3 cups = 750 mL
4 cups = 1 quart = 1 L

## VOLUME MEASUREMENTS (fluid)

1 fluid ounce (2 tablespoons) = 30 mL
4 fluid ounces ($1/2$ cup) = 125 mL
8 fluid ounces (1 cup) = 250 mL
12 fluid ounces ($1 1/2$ cups) = 375 mL
16 fluid ounces (2 cups) = 500 mL

## WEIGHTS (mass)

$1/2$ ounce = 15 g
1 ounce = 30 g
3 ounces = 90 g
4 ounces = 120 g
8 ounces = 225 g
10 ounces = 285 g
12 ounces = 360 g
16 ounces = 1 pound = 450 g

## DIMENSIONS

$1/16$ inch = 2 mm
$1/8$ inch = 3 mm
$1/4$ inch = 6 mm
$1/2$ inch = 1.5 cm
$3/4$ inch = 2 cm
1 inch = 2.5 cm

## OVEN TEMPERATURES

250°F = 120°C
275°F = 140°C
300°F = 150°C
325°F = 160°C
350°F = 180°C
375°F = 190°C
400°F = 200°C
425°F = 220°C
450°F = 230°C

## BAKING PAN SIZES

| Utensil | Size in Inches/Quarts | Metric Volume | Size in Centimeters |
|---|---|---|---|
| Baking or Cake Pan (square or rectangular) | 8×8×2 | 2 L | 20×20×5 |
| | 9×9×2 | 2.5 L | 23×23×5 |
| | 12×8×2 | 3 L | 30×20×5 |
| | 13×9×2 | 3.5 L | 33×23×5 |
| Loaf Pan | 8×4×3 | 1.5 L | 20×10×7 |
| | 9×5×3 | 2 L | 23×13×7 |
| Round Layer Cake Pan | 8×1½ | 1.2 L | 20×4 |
| | 9×1½ | 1.5 L | 23×4 |
| Pie Plate | 8×1¼ | 750 mL | 20×3 |
| | 9×1¼ | 1 L | 23×3 |
| Baking Dish or Casserole | 1 quart | 1 L | — |
| | 1½ quart | 1.5 L | — |
| | 2 quart | 2 L | — |